CHICKEN RUN

Cracked-Up

JOKE BOOK

by Louis Phillips

PUFFIN BOOKS

Published by the Penguin Group

Penguin Putnam Books for Young Readers, 345 Hudson Street,
New York, New York 10014, U.S.A.

Penguin Books Ltd, 27 Wrights Lane, London W8 5TZ, England

Penguin Books Australia Ltd, Ringwood, Victoria, Australia

Penguin Books Canada Ltd, 10 Alcorn Avenue, Toronto, Ontario, Canada M4V 3B2

Penguin Books (N.Z.) Ltd, 182-190 Wairau Road, Auckland 10, New Zealand

Penguin Books Ltd, Registered Offices: Harmondsworth, Middlesex, England

Published by Puffin Books,
a division of Penguin Putnam Books for Young Readers, 2000

5 7 9 10 8 6 4

TM & © 2000 DreamWorks,
Aardman Chicken Run Limited and Pathè Image
Jokes by Louis Phillips
All rights reserved

Puffin Books ISBN 0-14-130876-1

Printed in the United States of America

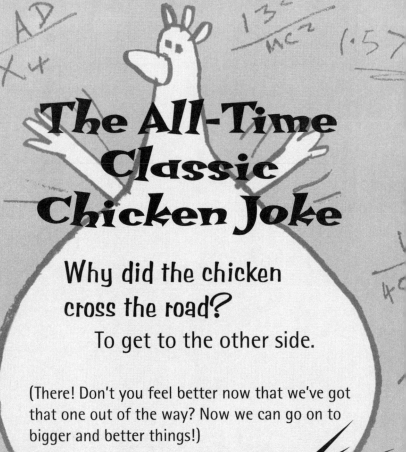

The All-Time Classic Chicken Joke

Why did the chicken cross the road?

To get to the other side.

(There! Don't you feel better now that we've got that one out of the way? Now we can go on to bigger and better things!)

Braaak!

How does an egg get to work?
It drives a yolkswagen.

NICK: What do you get when you dip a hen into a jar of peanut butter?

FETCHER: I don't know, but when you fry its eggs, they stick to the roof of your mouth.

MR. TWEEDY: I'm getting tired of chicken potpies. Can't we make an egg roll instead.

MRS. TWEEDY: How do you make an egg roll?

MR. TWEEDY: You push it, luv.

EGG #1: Knock, knock.
EGG #2: Who's there?
EGG #1: Omelet.
EGG #2: Omelet who?
EGG #1: Omelet smarter than I look.

How do ghosts like their eggs?
Terrorfried.

MRS. TWEEDY IN A RESTAURANT: Waiter, these eggs are too runny!
WAITER: Do you want to send them back to the chef?
MRS. TWEEDY: Too late! They've just run out the door.

MR. TWEEDY: Did you ever see an egg roll?
MRS. TWEEDY: No, but I've seen an apple turnover.

FETCHER: There was a farmer and he didn't have any hens and he never bought any eggs. And yet he had eggs every morning for breakfast. How?
NICK: He stole them.
FETCHER: Nope.
NICK: Then it's impossible.
FETCHER: Nope. He kept ducks and ate duck eggs instead.
NICK: As the French hens say—"Voila!"

NICK: Look at these beautiful eggs I swiped.

FETCHER: Wonderful.

NICK: I'll say.

FETCHER: I bet I can drop them three feet without breaking.

NICK: How is that possible?

FETCHER: Get on a ladder and drop them four feet. For the first three feet they won't break at all.

NICK: Hey, Fetcher, listen carefully.

FETCHER: I'm mostly ears.

NICK: There's a rooster on a roof. There is a west wind blowing 40 miles per hour. There is an east wind blowing 50 miles per hour. The rooster lays an egg on top of the roof. Which way will the egg roll—to the east side of the house or the west side of the house.

FETCHER: That's easy. To the west side.

NICK: Are you crazy? Roosters don't lay eggs!

GINGER: Why was Humpty-Dumpty such a disappointment?

ROCKY: He wasn't everything he was cracked up to be.

Mr. Tweedy, trying to escape from Mrs. Tweedy's cooking, goes into a restaurant to order breakfast. "I'll have two eggs," he tells the waiter. "I want one fried and one scrambled."

After a short wait, the waiter brings the eggs. Mr. Tweedy looks at them and says, "You scrambled the wrong one!"

BRAAAK!

BUNTY: How do you make an egg laugh?
BABS: Tell it a yolk.

NICK: An egg and a rooster ran a race. Who won?
FETCHER: I don't know, who won?
NICK: Well, the egg got beaten.

How many rotten eggs does it take to make a stink bomb?

A phew.

GINGER: Who was the most famous egg in American History?
ROCKY: Eggs Benedict Arnold.

gseg = scrambled eggs.

NICK: Do you know the difference between a
    dozen elephants and a dozen eggs?
FETCHER: No, I don't.
NICK: Then I'm not sending you to the store
    to buy a dozen eggs.

MAC: Why did Humpty-Dumpty have a
    great fall?
BABS: Why?
MAC: To make up for a terrible spring.

BUNTY (ON THE PHONE TO THE FIRE DEPARTMENT): Come
    quickly. The henhouse is on fire!
FIRE CHIEF: Okay. How do I get there?
BUNTY: Don't you still have that big red truck?

Fowler, Babs, and Bunty were arguing about the
sun and where it came from when it rose in the
morning. They argued and argued and argued.
    Finally, the answer dawned on them.

BABS: What did the rooster say to the furniture polisher at 5 a.m.?

BUNTY: Rise and shine! Rise and shine!

FOWLER: How come chickens have feathers all over their bodies?

BUNTY: How come?

FOWLER: If a chicken didn't have feathers, he wouldn't be a chicken. He'd be a little bare.

BUNTY: Where do chickens go for a vacation?

FOWLER: Where?

BUNTY: To Chick-ago.

NICK: What do you get if you cross a pig with a rooster?

FETCHER: You get an animal that goes "Oink-a-doodle-doo!"

GINGER: I've got a riddle for you.

FOWLER: Go ahead! Shoot.

GINGER: What has feathers, lays eggs, is white, then purple, then white, then purple.

FOWLER: My cranium is bursting with ignorance.

GINGER: A simple "I don't know" would suffice.

FOWLER: Okay. I give up. What has feathers, lays eggs, is white, then purple, then white, then purple.

GINGER: A hen working part-time as an egg-plant.

BUNTY: Crikey! I just swallowed a pumpkin seed.

FOWLER: Don't worry about it. You'll be vine.

NICK: What goes "Kaaaarb, kaaaarb, kaaaarb, kaaaarb"?

FETCHER: What?

NICK: A hen talking backward.

GINGER: What do you get if you cross a hen with a parrot?

BRAAAK!

ROCKY: You get a bird that lays an egg and then brags about it.

ROCKY: Hey, doll face.

GINGER: The name is Ginger!

ROCKY: Well, Ginger. What do you think about rats?

GINGER: Ah, they act like gnaw-it-alls.

ROCKY: Is there a problem here?

BUNTY: No. I'm just reading how all the cows on the neighboring farm are sick.

ROCKY: What's wrong with them?

BUNTY: Crikey, they're suffering from moo-laria.

BUNTY: I'm stuck! I forgot my lines!
ROCKY: Try winging it.

What did the hen say to the famous actor before
he went on stage?

Braaaak a leg.

Why does Mr. Tweedy place his hands over his
ears before entering the henhouse?

Because he can't stand to listen to fowl
language.

FOWLER: What happened to the rooster who broke into the Italian restaurant?

GINGER: What is it with me and roosters?

FOWLER: Codswallop! Just answer the question, please!

GINGER: Okay, what happened to the rooster who broke into the Italian restaurant?

FOWLER: That doesn't answer the question. That asks the question!

GINGER: Braak!

FOWLER: Okay, I'll tell you what happened to the rooster who broke into the Italian restaurant. He got arrested for disturbing the pizza.

NICK: What did the chicken say to the miser counting his money?

FETCHER: "Cheep, cheep, cheep!"

FOWLER: Why are the chickens sick?

BUNTY: I think they've come down with people pox.

ROCKY: **What has 2 arms, 2 wings, 2 tails, 3 heads, 3 bodies, and 8 legs?**

GINGER: **I give up.**

ROCKY: **A man on a horse holding a chicken.**

MR. TWEEDY: **Why are you going around town telling everybody I'm an idiot?**

MRS. TWEEDY: **I'm sorry. Is it supposed to be a secret?**

MAC: **Which side of a chicken has the most feathers?**

BUNTY: **I don't know, which side?**

MAC: **The outside!**

MRS. TWEEDY: Our profits are getting away. Why aren't our hens laying any eggs?

MR. TWEEDY: Maybe they're tired of working for chicken feed.

ROCKY: What does a rooster use to get up so early in the morning?

FOWLER: An alarm cluck.

Latest survey shows that 3 out of 4 chickens make up 75% of the world's chicken population.

What do you get when you cross a chicken with a giant ape on top of the Empire State Building?

Chicken a la Kong.

FETCHER: What did the hen say when she fell down the chimney?

NICK: What?

FETCHER: Soots me fine.

ROCKY: Knock, knock.
BABS: Who's there?
ROCKY: Highway cop.
BABS: Highway cop who?
ROCKY: Highway cop
   everybody at dawn when
   I go "Cock-a-doodle-doo."

FETCHER: Who's the most dangerous hen in the
   henhouse?
NICK: Attila the Hen.

MAC: What is a baby chicken's favorite
   game?
GINGER: What?
MAC: Beak-a-boo.

MAC: **What is a rooster's favorite movie?**
ROCKY: **You mean besides *Chicken Run*?**
MAC: **Yeah. Besides *Chicken Run*.**
ROCKY: **What?**
MAC: ***That's Hentertainment!***

FETCHER: **What do you get if you cross a chicken with a bell?**
GINGER: **What?**
FETCHER: **A chicken that wrings its own neck.**

ROCKY: **I'm looking for Ginger. Do you know where I can get hold of her?**
MAC: **I don't know. She's awfully ticklish.**

ROCKY: My cousin's with the FBI.

GINGER: That's impressive.

ROCKY: Yeah. They caught him in Chicago.

MAC: I played the greatest practical joke on Mr. Tweedy.

GINGER: What did you do?

MAC: Six months ago, I changed the taps on his bathtub so that the hot water would come out of the faucet marked cold and cold water would flow out of the faucet marked hot.

GINGER: Was Mr. Tweedy angry?

MAC: He will be when he finds out.

BABS: Did you hear that Mr. Tweedy was once in barber college?

MAC: No. What happened?

BABS: He was expelled for cutting classes.

BABS: Poor Bunty! She just ate a bag of cement.

MAC: What's going to become of her?

BABS: I guess she'll take up brick laying.

BABS: What are you going to do when you escape from the henhouse?

ROCKY: I once worked for the circus. I think I'll go back.

BABS: What did you do there?

ROCKY: I was The Rooster Cannonball. I was shot out of a cannon.

BABS: How was it?

ROCKY: Not so good. I got fired all the time.

MAC: What's wrong with Ginger today?

BABS: She ran over herself.

MAC: Ran over herself? Why that's impossible!

BABS: No. She asked Rocky to bring back some suspenders, but he couldn't go, so she ran over herself.

ROCKY: I keep thinking about monorails.

GINGER: That's because you have a one-track mind.

ROCKY: Did you hear about the pig who ended up in the pigpen?

GINGER: No. What happened?

ROCKY: She had a swill time.

BUNTY: Last night I had the strangest dream. I
dreamt I was a muffler on a Volkswagen.

GINGER: And then what happened?

BUNTY: I woke up *exhausted*.

BABS: Moo, moo.

MAC: What do you mean "Moo, moo"? You're
supposed to go "cluck, cluck."

BABS: I know, but I've decided to study a foreign
language.

GINGER: What do you think the sun is made of?

BABS: The sun must be made of yeast.

GINGER: Why do you say that?

BABS: Because it rises every morning.

FETCHER: What do you call a chicken ghost?

NICK: A poultrygeist.

GINGER: Rocky, will you remember who I am tomorrow?

Eggciting

ROCKY: Of course I shall.

GINGER: Will you remember who I am next week?

ROCKY: Don't worry your pretty little head about it. Of course I'll remember you.

GINGER: Will you remember me forever and ever?

ROCKY: Absolutely, doll face. How could I ever forget you?

GINGER: Knock, knock.

ROCKY: Who's there?

GINGER: Ginger.

ROCKY: Ginger who?

GINGER: See? You've forgotten me already.

FOWLER: Where have you been?

ROCKY: I just returned from playing tennis with a team from Africa.

FOWLER: Zulus?

ROCKY: No. Actually I won.

ROCKY: Look at those two snails fighting.
GINGER: Shouldn't you break them up?
ROCKY: Naah. Let them slug it out.

ROCKY: Does Ginger bite?
GINGER: No. Ginger snaps.

BABS: Knock, knock.
MAC: Who's there?
BABS: Abby.
MAC: Abby who?
BABS: Abby birthday to you.

GINGER: Knock, knock.
ROCKY: Who's there?
GINGER: Norma Lee.
ROCKY: Norma Lee who?
GINGER: Norma Lee, I don't go
out with roosters like you.

USDA Certified
Eggstra
Wacky

OMELET – Famous Shakespearean play about an egg that wanted to avenge its father's death.

Braaak!

GINGER: Where do you bathe?
ROCKY: I bathe in the spring.
GINGER: I said where, not when.

BABS: I haven't slept in six days.
BUNTY: Gracious. You must be exhausted.
BABS: Naah. I sleep in the nights.

ROCKY: Did you hear the joke about the jump rope?

GINGER: No. How how does it go?

ROCKY: Skip it.

ROCKY: Can I see you pretty soon?

GINGER: Why? Aren't I pretty now?

GINGER: Where shall we meet?

BUNTY: Meet me by the clothesline.

GINGER: Why the clothesline?

BUNTY: Because that's where I hang out.

BABS: Knock, knock.

FOWLER: Who's there?

BABS: Ammonia.

FOWLER: Ammonia who?

BABS: Ammonia bird in a gilded cage.

ROCKY: Would you like to take a walk?

GINGER: I'd love to.

ROCKY: Well, don't let me stop you.

MR. TWEEDY: What do you get when you cross a
    rooster with a woodpecker?
MRS. TWEEDY: What?
MR. TWEEDY: A bird that knocks on your
    door to wake you up.

Eggsclusive

ROCKY: Knock, knock.
GINGER: Who's there?
ROCKY: I am.
GINGER: I am who?
ROCKY: I am Rocky. I thought you knew
    that by now.

GINGER: Rocky, I've changed my mind.
ROCKY: Good. Does it work better now?

ROCKY: I can lift an elephant with one hand.
GINGER: Now you're bragging!
ROCKY: No, I'm not. Just find me an elephant
    that has one hand and I'll lift it in a minute.

BUNTY: Did you hear that Mrs. Tweedy is
    teaching the chickens how to bowl?
MAC: Oh, spare me!

MR. TWEEDY: What do you get when you cross a chicken with an octopus?

MRS. TWEEDY: What?

MR. TWEEDY: Enough drumsticks for everyone in the entire family!

NICK: What do you get when you cross a chicken with an elephant?

FETCHER: What?

NICK: A very cross chicken.

MR. TWEEDY: What famous chicken said, "Give me liberty or give me death"?

MRS. TWEEDY: Who?

MR. TWEEDY: Patrick HENry.

MR. TWEEDY (IN A FANCY RESTAURANT): I would like to order the special chicken soup.

WAITER: Certainly, sir. What kind of soup would the special chicken like?

MR. TWEEDY: How long is it possible for a human being to live without a brain?

MRS. TWEEDY: I don't know. How old are you?

MR. TWEEDY: If you can guess how many chickens I have in my sack, I'll give you both of them.

MRS. TWEEDY: What goes "ha ha ha plop"?
MR TWEEDY: What?
MRS. TWEEDY: A chicken laughing its head off.

NICK: Who gets up earlier—
   a chicken or a duck?
FETCHER: A chicken?
NICK: No, the duck.
FETCHER: Why the duck?
NICK: Because ducks get up at the quack of dawn.

BRAAAK!

MR. TWEEDY: I think I'll give up chicken farming
   and learn to sharpen knives and scissors.
MRS. TWEEDY: Don't do it.
MR. TWEEDY: Why not?
MRS. TWEEDY: Because you'll find everything
   much too dull.

MRS. TWEEDY: I'm going to go review the accounts
   in the orange juice factory.
MR. TWEEDY: Why are you going to the orange
   juice factory?
MRS. TWEEDY: So I can concentrate.

MR. TWEEDY: What's better than a dead chicken?
MRS. TWEEDY: Nothing.

MRS. TWEEDY: I just hired a scientist to clone my
rooster.
MR. TWEEDY: How does the rooster feel?
MRS. TWEEDY: He's beside himself.

NICK: Why can't chickens sing like other birds?
FETCHER: Why?
NICK: Because they don't know the words!

MRS TWEEDY: What seems to be the problem today?
MR. TWEEDY: I'm reading this article in the
newspaper and I need to know the difference
between being uninformed and being
apathetic.
MRS. TWEEDY: That's what you want to know, is it?
MR. TWEEDY: Yes, dear.
MRS. TWEEDY: Well, I don't know and I don't care.

FETCHER: If you can guess how many eggs I have
in my sack, I'll give you both of them.

MR. TWEEDY: Those oysters I ate for supper are making my stomach ache.

MRS. TWEEDY: Were the oysters fresh?

MR. TWEEDY: I'm not sure.

MRS. TWEEDY: Well, how did they look to you when you opened the shells?

MR. TWEEDY: Opened the shells?

MR. TWEEDY: I like spaghetti with baked chicken.

MRS. TWEEDY: I know you do.

MR. TWEEDY: Who do you think invented spaghetti?

MRS. TWEEDY: Someone who was using his noodle.

MRS. TWEEDY: How do my pancakes taste?

MR. TWEEDY: Hmmm.

MRS. TWEEDY: You can tell me the truth.

MR. TWEEDY: All right, your pancakes taste waffle.

MRS. TWEEDY: Where did all the fleas go?

MR. TWEEDY: Search me.

MRS. TWEEDY: I'd prefer not to.

MR. TWEEDY: What are the police doing to the criminal chickens?

MRS. TWEEDY: Grilling them, I hope.

MAC: I just received an anonymous letter.

BABS: Who's it from?

MR. TWEEDY: This chicken soup tastes funny.

MRS. TWEEDY: Then why aren't you laughing?

MRS. TWEEDY: What do you get when you cross a chicken with an octopus?

MR. TWEEDY: I give up. What?

MRS. TWEEDY: Eight feather dusters.

BRAAAK!

MR. TWEEDY: I love that tree we planted
in the barnyard.

MRS. TWEEDY: I do too.

MR. TWEEDY: Do you think we'll
get a lot of apples off it soon?

MRS. TWEEDY: I doubt it.

MR. TWEEDY: Why do you doubt it?

MRS. TWEEDY: Because it's a pear tree.

MR. TWEEDY: I think I would like chicken chili
instead of chicken potpies.

MRS. TWEEDY: How do you make chicken chili?

MR. TWEEDY: Take them to the North Pole.

MRS. TWEEDY: Why is this chicken potpie all
smashed?

MR. TWEEDY: Didn't you tell me to make you a pie
and step on it?

MR. TWEEDY: I'm tired of chicken potpies. Today I
think I'll make an apple turnover.

MRS. TWEEDY: How do you make an apple turnover?

MR. TWEEDY: I guess I'll tickle its stomach.

MRS. TWEEDY: We have to buy another watchdog to guard the henhouse.

MR. TWEEDY: So go to the pet store.

MRS. TWEEDY: But the dogs are so expensive. Do you think there are any dogs that will go cheap?

MR. TWEEDY: No, I'm sure they'll all go "woof, woof."

MRS. TWEEDY: I want to know how all our chickens escaped.

MR. TWEEDY: I have no idea.

MRS. TWEEDY: But I told you to guard all the exits.

MR. TWEEDY: Maybe they escaped through the entrances.

MRS. TWEEDY: The news on television says that our part of town may experience an earthquake tonight.

MR. TWEEDY: It's not my fault!

MRS. TWEEDY: Can you help me, doctor? My husband thinks he's a chicken.

DOCTOR: How long has he been acting like a chicken?

MRS. TWEEDY: Six or seven months.

DOCTOR: Why didn't you come to me sooner?

MRS. TWEEDY: We needed the eggs.

MRS. TWEEDY: What do you call a chicken that has no feathers?

MR. TWEEDY: What?

MRS. TWEEDY: Dinner.

Eggciting

ROCKY: Can I hear the joke about the henhouse roof?

GINGER: No.

ROCKY: Why not?

GINGER: Because it's over your head.

BUNTY: Can I hear the joke about the fifteen-foot fence?

MAC: No.

BUNTY: Why not?

MAC: Because you'll never get over it.

MR. TWEEDY: For supper, why don't I make some backward cheese.

MRS. TWEEDY: What kind of cheese is made backward?

MR. TWEEDY: Edam.

MR. TWEEDY: I have a headache.

MRS. TWEEDY: Well, stick your head through the window.

MR. TWEEDY: How will that help?

MRS. TWEEDY: It will make the pane go away.

MRS. TWEEDY: Why are you covered with bruises?

MR. TWEEDY: I started to go out through a revolving door.

MRS. TWEEDY: So?

MR. TWEEDY: And then I changed my mind.

FARMHAND: Come quick! Mrs. Tweedy just fell down the wishing well.
MR. TWEEDY: Ah! It works!

NICK: What has steel on the outside, feathers on the inside, and is extremely dangerous?
FETCHER: I'm rowing with no oars in the water. Tell me.
NICK: A chicken in an armored tank.

MR. TWEEDY: There's a man at the door collecting for the community swimming pool.
MRS. TWEEDY: Okay. Give him a glass of water.

MRS. TWEEDY: Time for your violin lesson.
MR. TWEEDY: Oh, fiddle.

MR. TWEEDY: What are you making for supper?

MRS. TWEEDY: A UFO.

MR. TWEEDY: What's a UFO?

MRS. TWEEDY: An Unidentified Frying Object.

MR. TWEEDY: What's this fly doing in my chicken soup?

MRS. TWEEDY: Let me look.

MR. TWEEDY (POINTING): See?

MRS. TWEEDY: Looks like it's doing the backstroke.

BUNTY: Can you tell me the joke about the broken pencil?

MAC: No.

BUNTY:
Why not?

MAC: It doesn't have any point.

MRS. TWEEDY: Why are you placing lights around the sundial?

MR. TWEEDY: So I can tell time at night.

FETCHER: At the zoo, I saw a man-eating tiger.

NICK: Big deal! This morning I saw a man eating chicken.

NICK: What do you get when you cross a chicken with a general?

FETCHER: What?

NICK: A new pecking order.

BRAAAK!

MRS. TWEEDY: Mr. Tweedy! What are you doing in the sink?

MR. TWEEDY: I want to learn tap dancing.

MRS. TWEEDY: I have to pay all these bills. Could you please address these envelopes for me?

MR. TWEEDY: Okay. Hello, envelopes.

NICK: I'm going to invent the wheel.

FETCHER: That should cause a revolution.

NICK: My uncle swallowed a pound of chicken feathers.

FETCHER: What happened to him?

NICK: He was tickled to death.

ROCKY: I just got an idea!

GINGER: Beginner's luck.

NICK: Is chicken soup really good for your health?
FETCHER: Not if you're a chicken.

NICK: What do you get if you light dynamite in
the henhouse?
FETCHER: What?
NICK: A big eggs-plosion!

NICK: What do you get if you cross a hen
with a dog?
FETCHER: What?
NICK: Pooched eggs.

Eggsclusive

MRS. TWEEDY: How do you
stop a rooster from crowing on Sunday
morning?
MR. TWEEDY: How?
MRS. TWEEDY: Eat him on Saturday night.

NICK: If you have 300 hens and 50 roosters,
what do you have?
FETCHER: What?
NICK: Enough eggs to make the largest
omelet in the world.

BUNTY: How do hens and roosters dance?
FOWLER: How?
BUNTY: Chick to chick.

ROCKY: What kind of dance do hens like the least?
GINGER: What?
ROCKY: The fox-trot.

BRAAAK!

FETCHER: What kinds of
    entertainers tell chicken jokes?
NICK: What kind?
FETCHER: Comedi-hens.

MRS. TWEEDY: When is the best time to buy baby
    chickens?
MR. TWEEDY: When?
MRS. TWEEDY: When they're going cheep.

NICK: Isn't that the height of stupidity?

FETCHER: What's the height of stupidity?

NICK: I don't know. How tall are you?

BUNTY: Did you hear about the fifty-year-old egg?

MAC: No. What about it?

BUNTY: Oh, it's a very old yolk.

NICK: Who is a hen's favorite movie actor?
FETCHER: I give up.
NICK: Gregory Peck peck peck.

FETCHER: What do you get when you cross a
magician with a chicken?
NICK: What?
FETCHER: Cheep tricks.

FETCHER: I'm hungry.

NICK: I know someplace where we can eat dirt cheap.

FETCHER: I know, but I don't want to eat dirt.

NICK: Then let's eat up the road.

FETCHER: No, thanks. I don't like the taste of asphalt.

MR. TWEEDY: I don't know what's wrong with me. My tongue's been sticking out all day long.

MRS. TWEEDY: Hold still. I have lots of stamps that need licking.

NICK: What has two feet, feathers all over its body, and barks like a dog?

FETCHER: What?

NICK: A chicken.

FETCHER: But a chicken doesn't bark like a dog.

NICK: I know. I just put that in to make it harder.

NICK: Where are you going?

FETCHER: I'm going to fetch some suspenders and a henway.

NICK: What's a henway?

FETCHER: Oh, three to four pounds.

NICK: Do you know that Mr. Tweedy once worked
for the telephone company, but he was fired?

FETCHER: That's too bad.

NICK: Yes. He missed his calling.

NICK: Let's grill some hamburgers.

FETCHER: How do you grill hamburgers?

NICK: First, you read them their rights.

MRS. TWEEDY: What do you have to know to
teach a chicken tricks?

MR. TWEEDY: What?

MRS. TWEEDY: More than the
chicken.

Fresh

MAC: What's blue and goes "cluck, cluck, cluck"?

BABS: What?

MAC: A chicken at the North Pole.

BABS (RUNNING TO THE VETERINARIAN): Doctor, doctor.
Help me! I'm shrinking.

VETERINARIAN: Oh, be a little patient.

MAC: What are you doing with all that steel wool?

BABS: I'm going to knit myself a tank.

BABS: Look at me! There's a cabbage growing out of the top of my head.

MAC: That's terrible.

BABS: Yes. Especially because I planted rutabaga.

BABS: What is five Q and five Q?

MAC: Ten Q.

BABS: You're welcome.

BABS: Guess what I saw today?

MAC: What?

BABS: Everything I looked at.

FOWLER: What has eighteen legs and catches flies?

ROCKY: A baseball team?

FOWLER: Naah. Nine chickens armed with swatters.

MAC: Gee, Babs, how did you get that awful
    bump on your beak?

BABS: I stopped to smell the broses.

MAC: Broses? There's no *b* in *roses*.

BABS: There was in the one I smelled.

MAC: I know a chicken that sounds exactly like an owl.

BABS: Who?

MAC: Make that two chickens....

BRAAAK!

GINGER: I'm not feeling well. I've got to see a doctor.

ROCKY: Which doctor?

GINGER: No. I'd prefer one with a medical license.

BABS: What's the best way to get rid of a 1,000-pound worm?

MAC: How?

BABS: Bring in a 2,000-pound chicken.

BABS: Bloomin' 'eck, I just swallowed a roll of film.
ROCKY: Stand still until we see what develops.

BABS: How do I get out of this henhouse?
MAC: Just go where the sign says "Eggs-it."

BABS: I just wrote a letter to my cousin. What should I do with it?
MAC: That's easy. Put it in an hen-velope.

BABS: I just found a four-leaf clover behind the henhouse.
BUNTY: It's all wrinkled.
BABS: Do you think I should iron it?
BUNTY: No. Don't press your luck.

MAC: How do you make a chicken sophisticated?
BABS: How?
MAC: Take away the *k* and *chick* becomes *chic*.

MAC: What's your favorite movie?
BABS: You mean besides *Chicken Run*?
MAC: Yeah.
BABS: *The Eggs-orcist.*

MAC: Do you want to hear about the rooster who went to the bowling alley?

BABS: I definitely do not.

MAC: Why not?

BABS: Because your mind is in the gutter.

NICK: Knock, knock.

FETCHER: Who's there?

NICK: Chickens go.

FETCHER: Chickens go who?

NICK: No they don't. Chickens go braak, braak.

BABS: Knock, knock.

MAC: Who's there?

BABS: Hatch.

MAC: Hatch who?

BABS: Gesundheit.

BUNTY: When is your birthday?

BABS: May 21st.

BUNTY: What year?

BABS: Every year.

MAC: Can you use the word hatchet in a sentence?

BABS: Ax me another question, please.

MAC: Go on. Try it.

BABS: Okay. A hen sits upon her egg to hatchet.

MAC: What do you think Rocky's worst fault is?

BUNTY: His vanity.

MAC: His vanity?

BUNTY: Yes. He likes to stand before a mirror to admire how handsome he is.

MAC: That's not vanity. That's having a vivid imagination.

BABS: Mac, help me! I'm losing my memory.

MAC: When did you first notice the problem?

BABS: What problem?

BABS: I think I'm going to run into a clothing store and throw a tantrum.

GINGER: Why inside a clothing store?

BABS: Isn't that a good place for fits?

MAC: Knock, knock.

BABS: Who's there?

MAC: Little old lady.

BABS: Little old lady who?

MAC: Aye, Babs, I didn't know you could yodel.

BRAAAK!

NICK: What's the difference between a crowd at a bullfight and a chicken farmer begging his hens to lay more eggs?

FETCHER: I give up. What?

NICK: The crowd shouts "Olé" while the farmer cries "Oh, lay!"

FOWLER: Maybe we should take flying lessons.

GINGER: No thanks. I don't believe in crash courses.

MAC: Do you want to hear a story about a ship that goes back and forth, back and forth, back and forth?

BABS: No.

MAC: Why not?

BABS: Because I don't believe in ferry tales.

BABS: I have a bad head cold. How can I prevent it from reaching my chest?

MAC: Tie a knot in your neck.

MAC: Did you hear about the silly hen who goes around saying "No"?

BABS: No.

MAC: Ah, well...

ROCKY: Will this path take me to the henhouse?

GINGER: No. You have to walk there.

NICK: Did you hear that Mrs. Tweedy gave her husband soap flakes for breakfast instead of corn flakes?

FETCHER: Was Mr. Tweedy mad?

NICK: Mad? He was foaming at the mouth.

MAC: Did you hear that Mr. Tweedy fell off the
     henhouse roof?

BABS: What did he say?

MAC: Should I leave out the bad words?

BABS: Yes.

MAC: Then he didn't say a thing.

BABS: If you don't mind waiting, I'll show you
     my new scarf.

MAC: How long?

BABS: About three feet.

BABS: An ant just crawled over my foot.

MAC: Which one?

BABS: I don't know. All ants look alike to me.

MAC: Did you see the watermelon patch?
BABS: Why? Are the watermelons leaking?

MAC: May I join you?
BABS: Why? Am I falling apart?

MAC: Does Mr. Tweedy talk to himself when he's alone?

BRAAAK!

BABS: I don't know. I've never been with him when he's alone.

Why did the chicken cross the playground?
   To get to the other slide.

Why did the turkey cross the road?
   It was stapled to the chicken.

What did the chicken do while it was praying?
   It crossed itself.

Why did the bubble gum cross the road?
   It was stuck to the chicken's left foot.

Why did the hen only go halfway across the road?
   Because she wanted to lay it on the line.

What do you call a chicken that crosses the road, falls into a mud puddle, and then crosses the road again?

A dirty double-crosser.

BUNTY: How do I get to the other side of the road?
MAC: You are on the other side.

GINGER: Why did the cow cross the road?
BUNTY: Why?
GINGER: To get to the udder side.

BABS: Why did the chicken cross the road?
BUNTY: To get to the other side?
BABS: No. To get *The Beijing Daily News.*
BUNTY: To get *The Beijing Daily News?*
BABS: You don't get it?
BUNTY: No. I don't get it at all.
BABS: Neither do I. I usually get *The New York Times.*

THE
CHICKEN RUN
READING LIST

1. **COOKING SECRETS** by Barbie Cue
2. **HOW TO FRY YOUR SUPPER** by Chris P. Chicken
3. **HOW TO ROPE CATTLE IN YOUR SPARE TIME** by Larry Ott
4. **LIVING BY YOURSELF IN THE BARNYARD** by I. Malone
5. **DELICIOUS SOUP** by Chick N. Noodle
6. **PUTTING SUNTAN LOTION ON YOUR CHICKEN**
   by Justin Casey Burns
7. **HOW TO WRITE THE GREAT CHICKEN EPIC**
   by Adeline Moore
8. **MOVING YOUR HENS ACROSS THE RIVER**
   by Carrie M. Hover
9. **THE LAZIEST CHICKEN WORKERS ON THE FARM**
   by Hans Dolittle
10. **PAIN IN THE HENHOUSE** by Anne Guish
11. **SCALP DISORDERS IN ROOSTERS** by Dan Druff
12. **MUSIC TO LAY EGGS BY** by Cass Ette
13. **THE CHICKEN CROSSES THE ROAD** by Luke Bothways
14. **THE GREAT CHICKEN MURDER MYSTERY**
    by Hugh Dunnit